Writing Workbook for Kids with Dyslexia

100 activities to improve writing and reading skills of dyslexic children

VOLUME 10

Brain Child

Copyright 2021 - All Rights Reserved

Contents of this book may not be reproduced, duplicated or transmitted without direct written permission from the author.
Under no circumstances will any legal responsibility or blame be held against the publisher for any reparation, damages or monetary loss due to information herein, either directly or indirectly.

Legal Notice:

You cannot amend, distribute, sell, use, quote or paraphrase any part of the contents within this book without the constent of the author.

Disclaimer Notice:

Please note that the information contained within this document serves only for educationaly entertainment purposes. No warranties of any kind are expressed or implied. Readers acknowledge that the author is not engaging in the rendering of legal, financial, medical or professional advice.

Table of contents

Page No.

1. Introduction ....
2. *Unit 1*: Syllabic Awareness Exercises ....
   - Activity 1: Syllabication rules 1
   - Activity 2: Listen and write 2
   - Activity 3: Mark the syllables 3
   - Activity 4: Say, clap, sort 4
3. *Unit 2*: Omission of syllables ....
   - Activity 1: Remove the 2ⁿᵈ syllable 5
   - Activity 2: Remove the 2ⁿᵈ syllable 6
   - Activity 3: Remove the 2ⁿᵈ syllable 7
   - Activity 4: Remove the 2ⁿᵈ syllable 8
4. *Unit 3*: Substitution of syllables ....
   - Activity 1: Use the syllable "aw" 9
   - Activity 2: Use the syllable "in" 10
   - Activity 3: Use the syllable "go" 11
   - Activity 4: Use the syllable "os" 12
5. *Unit 4*: Find the orally hidden syllables ....
   - Activity 1: Write syllable "tion" 13
   - Activity 2: Hidden syllable "ssion" 14
   - Activity 3: Missing syllable "cian" 15
   - Activity 4: Write syllable "el" 16

Table of contents

Page No.

6. *Unit 5*: Identify the repeated syllables ....
   - Activity 1: Circle the picture 17
   - Activity 2: Circle the letter 18
   - Activity 3: Write two different words 19
   - Activity 4: Write two different words 20

7. *Unit 6*: Chain of words ....
   - Activity 1: Make a chain of words 21
   - Activity 2: Make a chain of words 22
   - Activity 3: Game I-see I-see 23
   - Activity 4: Write the syllables 24

8. *Unit 7*: Order the syllables to form words ....
   - Activity 1: Form a word 25
   - Activity 2: Order the syllable 26
   - Activity 3: Name of shapes 27
   - Activity 4: Name of transportation 28

7. *Unit 8*: Complete words with syllables ....
   - Activity 1: Fill ups 29
   - Activity 2: Fill ups 30
   - Activity 3: Fill ups with syllable 31
   - Activity 4: Fill ups with syllable 32

8. *Unit 9*: Phoneme segmentation ....
   - Activity 1: How many letters 33

Table of contents

Page No.

Activity 2: How many letters	34
Activity 3: Counting of words	35
Activity 4: Counting of words	36

9. *Unit 10*: Phoneme skipping

Activity 1: Remove the 2nd sound	37
Activity 2: Words help box	38
Activity 3: Matching words	39
Activity 4: Color the box	40

10. *Unit 11*: Phoneme substitution

Activity 1: Replace the sound with "t"	41
Activity 2: Replace the sound with "p"	42
Activity 3: Replace the sound with "e"	43
Activity 4: Replace the sound with "f"	44

11. *Unit 12*: Find the hidden sounds

Activity 1: Write hidden phoneme	45
Activity 2: Write hidden phoneme	46
Activity 3: Find same phoneme sound	47
Activity 4: Write same phoneme sound	48

12. *Unit 13*: Auditory sound discrimination

Activity 1: Find "a" sound pictures	49
Activity 2: Find "g" sound pictures	50
Activity 3: Find "h" sound pictures	51

Table of contents

Page No.

    Activity 4: Find "r" sound pictures 52

13. *Unit 14*: Ordering graphemes to form words ....
    Activity 1: Order the letters 53
    Activity 2: Order the letters 54
    Activity 3: Order the letters 55
    Activity 4: Order the letters 56

14. *Unit 15*: Complete words with graphemes ....
    Activity 1: Fill in the blanks 57
    Activity 2: Fill in the blanks 58
    Activity 3: Fill in the blanks 59
    Activity 4: Fill in the blanks 60

15. *Unit 16*: Sound dictation ....
    Activity 1: What word am I naming? 61
    Activity 2: What word am I naming? 62
    Activity 3: What word am I naming? 63
    Activity 4: What word am I naming? 64

16. *Unit 17*: Mentally count the words ....
    Activity 1: Count the words in the sentence 65
    Activity 2: Count the words in the sentence 66
    Activity 3: Count and write 67
    Activity 3: Count and write 68

17. *Unit 18*: Omit a word in a sentence ....

Table of contents

Page No.

Activity 1: Remove the 3rd word	69
Activity 2: Remove the 3rd word	70
Activity 3: Remove the 3rd word	71
Activity 4: Remove the 3rd word	72

18. *Unit 19*: Substitute a word in a sentence
- Activity 1: Substitude the 3rd word with "cot" ... 73
- Activity 2: Substitude the 3rd word with "blue" ... 74
- Activity 3: Substitude the 3rd word with "pair" ... 75
- Activity 4: Substitude the 3rd word with "stop" ... 76

19. *Unit 20*: Separate written phrases into words
- Activity 1: Separate the words ... 77
- Activity 2: Separate the words ... 78
- Activity 3: Separate the words ... 79
- Activity 4: Separate the words ... 80

20. *Unit 21*: Binomial sentences
- Activity 1: "sick and tired" ... 81
- Activity 2: "short and sweet" ... 82
- Activity 3: "odds and ends" ... 83
- Activity 4: "back and forth" ... 84

21. *Unit 22*: Spelling exercises for words
- Activity 1: Compound words ... 85
- Activity 2: Compound words ... 86

Table of contents

                                                                                          Page No.

    Activity 3: Make and Write 87

    Activity 4: Make and Write 88

22. *Unit 23*: Activities with rhymes ....

    Activity 1: Rhyming words 89

    Activity 2: Rhyming words 90

    Activity 3: Find and mark 91

    Activity 4: Find and mark 92

23. *Unit 24*: Scrabble-type letters ....

    Activity 1: Word search 93

    Activity 2: Word search 94

    Activity 3: Crossword puzzle 95

    Activity 4: Crossword puzzle 96

24. *Unit 25*: Visual discrimination of syllables or graphemes ....

    Activity 1: Pictures of h and g 97

    Activity 2: Pictures of i and w 98

    Activity 3: Words with "ch" sound 99

    Activity 4: Words with "wh" sound 100

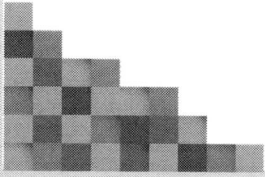

INTRODUCTION

Visit www.brainchildgrowth.com and download 25 free extra activities.

Dyslexia is a learning disorder. It can be said that a person is dyslexic when they have difficulties reading and understanding what is written.

When a child has dyslexia, it is much more difficult to decode the letters and read fluently. That is why these children often lose the thread of the class.

Dyslexia can be worked to improve the child's reading, writing and reading comprehension. The best way to work on these exercises with your child is to create a routine and work on one or two exercises each day.

Exercises to practice writing are covered in this volume and then a complementary activity to practice with the letters learned.

Never put excessive pressure on the child. Patience should be our word mantra. Keep in mind that for the child an exercise that you consider easy is very hard for them.

Focus on the child's small advances. Power your effort and less your results. Do everything you can so that they don't feel bad. Keep in mind that the child is making a great effort.

When we suspect that our child may be dyslexic, we can do a series of activities that will improve their literacy level. Whether in the end, the diagnosis is confirmed or discarded, it will still be very beneficial to facilitate their learning experience.

The important thing is to carry out this type of training before the age of 8 or 9, preferably during the last year of pre-school and the first year of Primary school, without taking into account that from school there is still no warning.

In any case, we cannot wait for the diagnosis to be confirmed because we will have missed the best time to intervene and prepare the child to learn to read, and we will have a serious problem if they start 3rd grade and we have not yet intervened the dyslexia, since the increase in school demands will make the problem visible.

In this book and the other volumes of BrainChild, you will find a multitude of resources to work with dyslexia both at school and at home. The exercises have been carried out under the supervision of psychologists and educators.

SYLLABICATION RULES

Rule 1: prefix and sufix
example - long/est   un/comfortable

Rule 2: VC/CV
example - tif/fin   hid/den

Rule 3: V/CV (long)
example - ro/bot   ba/sic

Rule 4: VC/V (short)
example - sev/en   trav/el

Rule 5: VC/CCV or VCC/CV
example - lob/ster   pump/kin

Rule 6: V/V
example - po/et   di/et

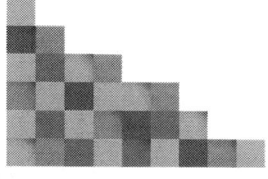

Syllabic Segmentation

Listen and write how many syllables are in each given word.

saturday		crossing	
children		captain	
climbing		reading	
internal		activity	
question		general	
father		blanket	
intelligent		composition	

Syllabic Segmentation

Say, clap, sort and mark the syllables for each word.

hospital	① ② ③	caterpillar	① ② ③
rainbow	① ② ③	trumpet	① ② ③
shirt	① ② ③	frog	① ② ③
xylophone	① ② ③	hotdog	① ② ③
crocodile	① ② ③	guitar	① ② ③

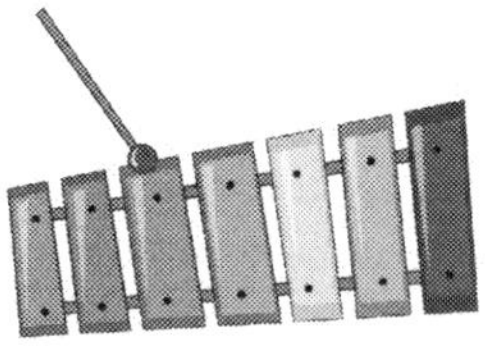

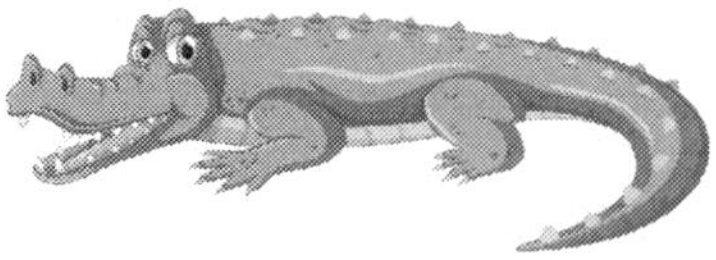

Syllabic Segmentation

Say, clap, sort and mark the syllables for each animal name.

 donkey ① ② ③	 fox ① ② ③
 pig ① ② ③	 tiger ① ② ③
 hen ① ② ③	 horse ① ② ③
 cow ① ② ③	 kangaroo ① ② ③
 koala ① ② ③	 sheep ① ② ③

Omission of Syllables

What would remain if we removed the 2nd syllable from the word?

above	abacus
aberration	abash
abandoned	abbreviation
abet	abut
absolute	abdicate

Omission of Syllables

What would remain if we remove the 2nd syllable from the word.

abode	abound
able	ablaze
abridge	abracadabra
ablaut	abolish
abaft	abrasion

Omission of Syllables

What would remain if we removed the 2nd syllable from the word?

abrupt	abnegate
accept	abominable
abrade	abeyance
abstract	about-turn
absence	application

Omission of Syllables

What would remain if we removed the 2nd syllable from the word?

ache	acid

active	actor

accurate	appeal

after	account

abstention	abstraction

What would remain if we removed the 2nd syllable from the word?

Substitution of Syllables

Replace the 2nd syllable of the word with the given syllable.

syllable - "aw"

bouncer	sponding
↓	↓
boawcer	

withdraw	burner
↓	↓

garment	bachelor
↓	↓

invention	helpless
↓	↓

Substitution of Syllables

Replace the 2nd syllable of the word with the given syllable.

syllable – "in"

important ↓	cover ↓
knife ↓	headscarf ↓
knowledge ↓	direction ↓
position ↓	company ↓

Substitution of Syllables

Replace the 2nd syllable of the word with the given syllable.

syllable – "go"

retained ↓	mowing ↓
empire ↓	continuous ↓
middle ↓	astringment ↓
remark ↓	accumulator ↓

Substitution of Syllables

Replace the 2nd syllable of the word with the given syllable.

syllable – "os"

reproduction ↓	agglomerate ↓
department ↓	specified ↓
disorderly ↓	aggrandize ↓
soreness ↓	grievance ↓

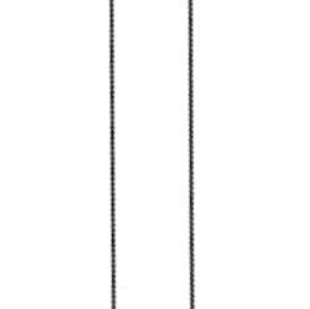

Find Orally hidden Syllables

Write the hidden syllable or piece that is missing in the word.

Write the missing syllable "tion"

dona__tion__

pollu____

attrac____

mo____

crea____

revolu____

ac____

opera____

loca____

vaca____

sta____

posi____

cau____

defini____

direc____

Find Orally hidden Syllables

Write the hidden syllable or piece that is missing in the word.

Write the missing syllable "ssion"

impre_____   percu_____   ingre_____

compa_____   remi_____

dismi_____   submi_____   conce_____

aggre_____   admi_____

profe_____   succe_____   omi_____

mi_____   pa_____

Find Orally hidden Syllables

15

Write the hidden syllable or piece that is missing in the word.

Write the missing syllable "cian"

magi_____ physi_____ opti_____

electri_____ clini_____

politi_____ statisti_____ techni_____

beauti_____ logi_____

patri_____ dieti_____ morti_____

clini_____ musi_____

Find Orally hidden Syllables

Write the hidden syllable or piece that is missing in the word.

Write the missing syllable "el"

bag__ canc__ parc__

gosp__ nick__

ang__ dies__ mod__

cru__ fu__

lab__ shov__ bush__

nov__ appar__

16

Identify repeated Syllables

Circle the picture that is different.

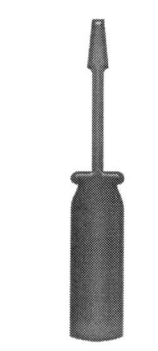   

Identify repeated Syllables

Circle the letter that is different.

18

W	W	W	R
D	D	G	D
Q	R	Q	Q
T	T	Y	T
J	X	J	J
E	H	E	E

Identify repeated Syllables

Write two different words in which syllables are repeated.

po	post	poster
fu		
sh		
th		
ea		
cr		
fo		
pa		
ye		
su		

Identify repeated Syllables

Write two different words in which syllables are repeated.

re	_____ _____
wa	_____ _____
qu	_____ _____
ze	_____ _____
da	_____ _____
bl	_____ _____
ic	_____ _____
fe	_____ _____
ru	_____ _____
ja	_____ _____

20

Word chain through Syllables

Write and make a chain of words through syllables.

nail	luck	kangaroo	octopus
early			
fruits			
roots			
slowly			
shape			
started			
bones			
useful			
distance			

Word chain through Syllables

22

Write and make a chain of words through syllables.

narrate			
gather			
producer			
nasal			
child			
quick			
laying			
learn			
farmer			
nacho			

Word chain through Syllables

I see–I see a little thing that begins with the letter.

I see–I see a little thing that begins with the letter "ca".

I see–I see a little thing that begins with the letter "ti".

I see–I see a little thing that begins with the letter "zu".

I see–I see a little thing that begins with the letter "te".

I see–I see a little thing that begins with the letter "sn".

Word chain through Syllables

24

Write and make a chain of words through syllables.

- crop
- pander
- hovel
- chickpeas
- goblet
- admired
- escape

Order the Syllables

Order the letters to form a word.

rrero	error	bkear	_____
	otca	_____	
lassg	_____	ostp	_____
	gsura	_____	
cklco	_____	pnceli	_____
	gndiaseo	_____	
viesde	_____	ckne	_____
	dloope	_____	
itrla	_____	ixngif	_____
	larif	_____	

25

Order the Syllables

Order the letters to form a word.

Scrambled	Answer	Scrambled	Answer
eltsopece	_____	techtra	_____
ootbh	_____		
fract	_____	ilfrl	_____
sthleru	_____		
caid	_____	eadl	_____
urpelp	_____		
oevm	_____	aecsh	_____
ribna	_____		
obmb	_____	gtilh	_____
lidfu	_____		

26

Order the Syllables

Order the letters to form the name of the shapes.

27

icrlec → circle	qreusa → _____
anlegtecr → _____	alvo → _____
rats → _____	oxagnehe → _____
ctoneoga → _____	uebc → _____
tagnepeno → _____	ylndierc → _____

Order the Syllables

Order the letters to form the name of the transportation.

ubs
↓
_____

ulacneamb
↓
_____

ihps
↓
_____

nva
↓
_____

piranlea
↓
_____

arc
↓
_____

tbao
↓
_____

ritna
↓
_____

ycbelci
↓
_____

ortmokibe
↓
_____

28

Complete words with Syllables

Fill in the blanks to complete words with letters.

a c t i o n	f _ si _ n	th _ ng	dr _ ve _
m _ tor	lea _ t	pl _ ce _	h _ me
ano _ _ er	four _ h	patt _ _ n	de _ _ h
va _ _ ey	d _ m _ ge	je _ t _ r	st _ ne
bu _ _ er	w _ nt _ r	sh _ _ e	l _ ye _

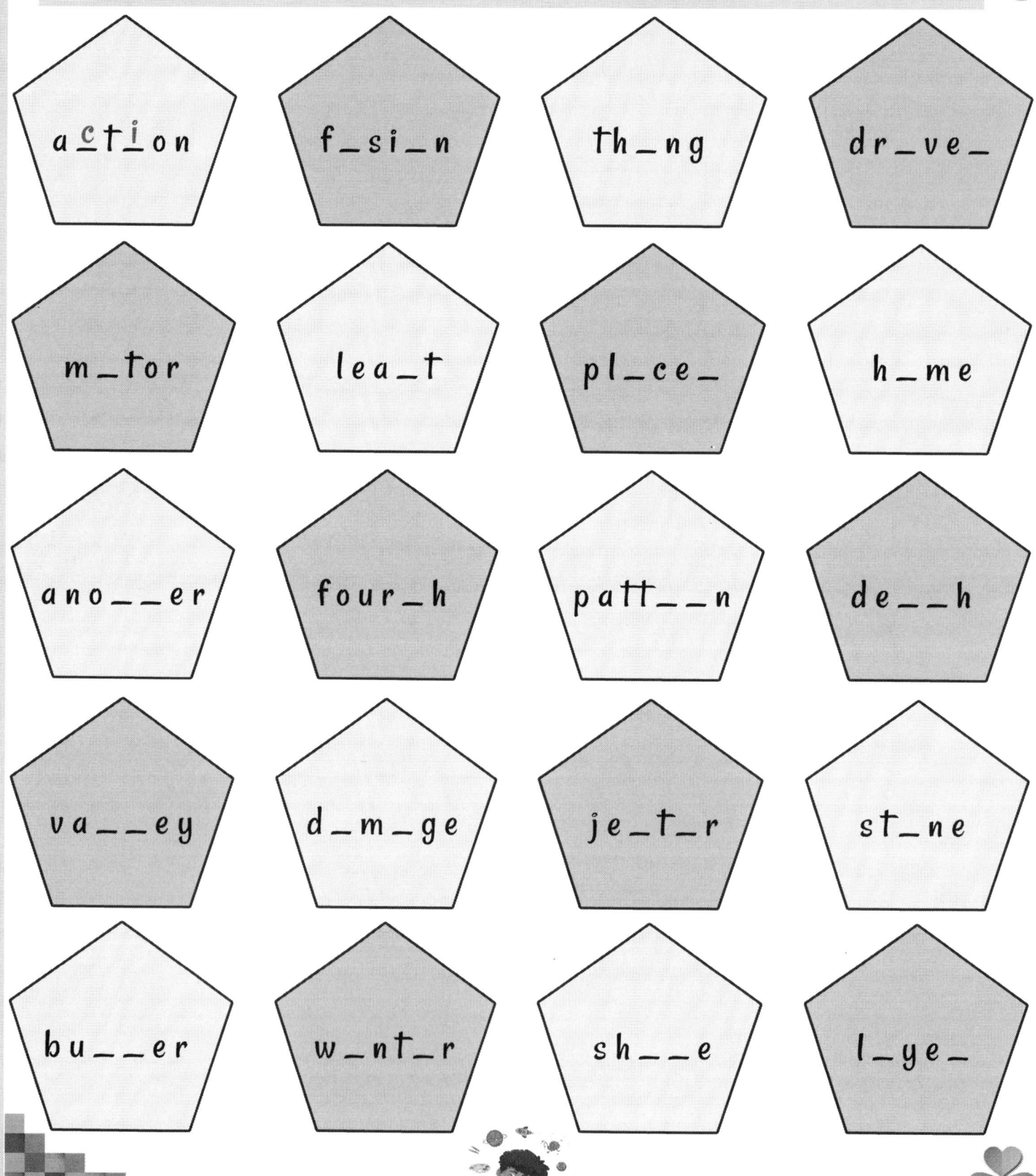

Complete words with Syllables

Fill in the blanks to complete words with letters.

30

f_rec_st	pr_v_de	p_lar	de___ver
pr_ng	pro_e_t	st_dy	co_pus
on_ar_	l_mp	patt___n	de___h
l_nd	off_ci_l	ch___p	r_v_r
c_ur_e	ev_nts	e_ce_s	ut_r_s

Complete words with Syllables

31

Fill in the blanks to complete the words with the correct syllables.

d a n c _e_ _r_

c l o _ _

b o _ _

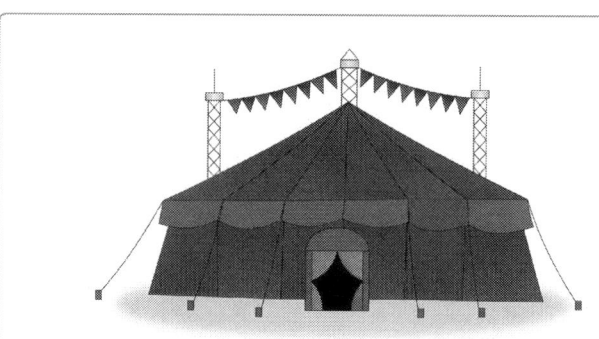

c i _ _ u s

c u p _ _ _ e

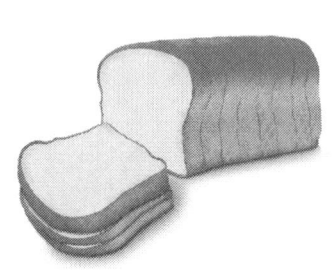

b r _ _ d

Complete words with Syllables

Fill in the blanks to complete the words with the correct syllables.

n u r _ _

o _ _ o p u s

h o _ _ e

m u s _ _ m

f i r e t _ _ _ k

j _ t

Phoneme Segmentation

Read and write how many letters the words have.

p r o f u s e
↓
p-r-o-f-u-s-e
(7)

w o l d
↓
_____
( )

t h e n c e
↓
_____
( )

t h e r m
↓
_____
( )

c l i m b i n g
↓
_____
( )

p o s h
↓
_____
( )

Phoneme Segmentation

Read and write how many letters the words have.

| s | h | o | w | i | n | g |

↓

_____

◯

| c | a | t | c | h |

↓

_____

◯

| p | e | r | s | o | n |

↓

_____

◯

| p | o | s | s | u | m |

↓

_____

◯

| m | u | t | a | t | i | o | n |

↓

_____

◯

| p | o | w | e | r |

↓

_____

◯

Phoneme Segmentation

Read and write how many letters the names of shapes have.

circle → c-i-r-c-l-e → 6

square → ___ → ☐

triangle → ___ → ☐

rectangle → ___ → ☐

star → ___ → ☐

pentagon → ___ → ☐

trapezoid → ___ → ☐

Phoneme Segmentation

Read and write how many letters the names of vegetables have.

potato → _____ → ☐

cabbage → _____ → ☐

peas → _____ → ☐

onion → _____ → ☐

broccoli → _____ → ☐

pumpkin → _____ → ☐

carrot → _____ → ☐

Phoneme Skipping

Write what would remain if we removed the 2nd letter from the given word.

special → secial	unique →	phrases →
catch →	verified →	general →
entries →	historical →	carefully →
technical →	literary →	visual →

Phoneme Skipping

38

Match with what would remain if we removed the 2nd letter from the given word.

sidecar		cildren
meridional		ehibition
exhibition		sdecar
tackle		frming
farming		tckle
century		cntury
children		mridional

Phoneme Skipping

Match with what would remain if we removed the 2nd letter from the given word.

authority	cromium
officer	rsolute
resolute	athority
sergeant	frming
chromium	ault
adult	sadium
stadium	srgeant

Phoneme Skipping

Remove the second letter from each word that is in a colored box. Find the resulting word in the white boxes and color it the same color as the original word.

uncrown — yellow

nurse — green

dmage

parallel — purple

damage — blue

sagehand

stagehand — pink

prallel

ucrown

nrse

Phoneme Substitution

Replace and write the 2nd sound of the words with "t".

41

incomplete ↓ itcomplete	uncured ↓	hyphenated ↓
likely ↓	filled ↓	intended ↓
usual ↓	raise ↓	express ↓
subdured ↓	obtained ↓	indicate ↓

Phoneme Substitution

Replace and write the 2nd letter of the words with " p ".

grounded ↓	relating ↓	emotionally ↓
behaved ↓	manners ↓	breeding ↓
wealthy ↓	deserved ↓	liberal ↓
whacked ↓	mammals ↓	customs ↓

Phoneme Substitution

Replace and write the 2nd letter of the words with " e ".

43

w a n a b e ↓	d e p a r t m e n t ↓	m o u s t a c h e ↓
f o u n d ↓	w a n t o n l y ↓	r a n k i n g ↓
m i s t r e s s ↓	w a r e h o u s e ↓	q u a n t i t y ↓
p a s s a g e ↓	s p e c i f y ↓	a d v a n c i n g ↓

Phoneme Substitution

Replace and write the 2nd letter of the words with "f".

token ↓	disease ↓	earlier ↓
regard ↓	poisonous ↓	disposed ↓
truth ↓	extreme ↓	incline ↓
edging ↓	establish ↓	influences ↓

Find the hidden sounds

What letter or phoneme sounds the same in the two given words?

t<u>ro</u>ugh	t<u>ro</u>uble	tro
reader	radium	
necessity	nefarious	
stringed	stroganoff	
zoo	zip	
voracious	vaudeville	
product	picture	
tuning	turn	
olive	oodles	
isolate	itemize	

Find the hidden sounds

Write the hidden phoneme or letter that is missing in the word.

is o metrics

goose_der

de_terium

kidne_

insta_ce

deter_inable

mati_ned

p_rification

Find the hidden sounds

Write the hidden phoneme or letter that is missing in the word.

bri_adier

st_eam

comma_ding

pect_ralis

additiona_

hormon_l

mo_sture

e_pelled

Find the hidden sounds

Write a word that has the same underlined letters or phoneme that sound the same.

<u>b</u>reath	<u>b</u>reast
<u>cl</u>ose	
<u>ho</u>use	
<u>a</u>venge	
<u>a</u>quatic	
<u>e</u>scalate	
<u>v</u>arying	
<u>s</u>equence	
<u>l</u>evel	
<u>p</u>erson	

48

Auditory sound discrimination

Circle the pictures that start with the " a " sound.

49

Auditory sound discrimination

Circle the pictures that start with the " g " sound.

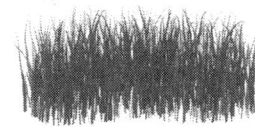

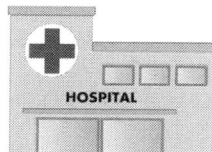

Auditory sound discrimination

Circle the pictures that start with the " h " sound.

Auditory sound discrimination

Circle the pictures that start with the " r " sound.

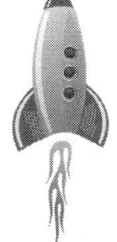

Ordering of Graphemes

Order the letters to form a word.

taolt → total

dnxei →

stra →

ecipe →

rmka →

vserei →

abcled →

ulipbc →

Ordering of Graphemes

54

Order the letters to form a word.

pcabela
↓

rmof
↓

vediesc
↓

mvoree
↓

tsnoe
↓

ergat
↓

lpnat
↓

cxudlee
↓

Ordering of Graphemes

Order the letters to form a word.

ounsd ↓	hrbus ↓
inev ↓	emnelte ↓
srgap ↓	vaido ↓
csepea ↓	knsi ↓

Ordering of Graphemes

Order the letters to form a word.

oels
↓

iulbd
↓

ortnf
↓

afel
↓

esvarle
↓

aseir
↓

ffero
↓

enalmt
↓

Complete words with Graphemes

Fill in the blanks to complete the word.

cet_a_cea

wha_e

mo_ify

walr_s

fea_ures

vi_ible

streaml_ned

bl_bber

th_ck

fore_imb

e_ternal

fl_ppers

Complete words with Graphemes

Fill in the blanks to complete the word.

l_bsters

seve_al

lar_est

th_rax

shri_ps

co_pound

cr_yfish

skel_ton

s_rface

abdo_en

thora_ic

appe_dages

Complete words with Graphemes

Fill in the blanks to complete the word.

st_ms

gr_und

tiss_es

shoo_

prote_tive

la_er

tou_h

api_al

tran_ports

ins_de

seco_dary

term_nal

Complete words with Graphemes

Fill in the blanks to complete the word.

60

per_od

donis_urs

mamm_ls

no_thern

expansi_n

fo_med

suit_d

nou_ish

contin_nts

tertia_y

com_ared

i_land

Dictation of Sounds

What word am I naming?

/p//a//r//t//n//e//r/	/m//i//l//l//i//o//n/
/w//a//t//e//r//p//r//o//o//f/	/f//o//r//e//s//t/
/e//x//t//i//n//c//t//i//o//n/	/a//n//i//m//a//l//s/
/s//h//a//l//l//o//w/	/h//e//m//i//s//p//h//e//r//e/
/l//o//c//k//e//d/	/c//l//i//m//a//t//e/

61

Dictation of Sounds

What word am I naming?

/m//o//u//n//t//a//i//n/ -	mountain
/s//e//d//i//m//e//n//t/ -	
/r//o//c//k/ -	
/o//c//e//a//n//i//c/ -	
/v//o//l//c//a//n//i//c/ -	
/p//u//s//h/ -	
/b//o//u//n//d//r//y/ -	
/f//a//u//l//t//l//i//n//e/ -	
/d//e//b//r//i//s/ -	

Dictation of Sounds

What word am I naming?

| /c//h//a//n//g//i//n//g/ | /d/r//i//f//t//i//n//g/ |

| /c//o//m//p//l//e/x/ | /w/o/r//n/ |

| /w//a/r//m//e/r/ | /g//l//a//c//i//a//l/ |

| /l//o//c//a//t//i//o/n/ | /s//p//e//c//i//e//s/ |

| /r//a//n//g//e//s/ | /g/l/o/b//a//l/ |

63

Dictation of Sounds

What word am I naming?

64

/p//o//w//e//r//f//u//l/   - _____

/n//e//u//t//r//o//n/   - _____

/s//t//u//d//y/   - _____

/d//i//a//m//e//t//e//r/   - _____

/r//e//m//a//i//n/   - _____

/s//w//e//e//p/   - _____

/h//o//r//i//z//o//n/   - _____

/g//r//a//v//i//t//y/   - _____

/f//o//r//m//a//t//i//o//n/ - _____

Mentally Count the Words

Write some sentences and count how many different words are in those sentences.

1.) The Earth is the third of the eight planets.
   1   2   3   4   5   6   7   8   9

   9 words

2.) _____

   _____

3.) _____

   _____

4.) _____

   _____

5.) _____

   _____

6.) _____

   _____

7.) _____

   _____

Mentally Count the Words

Write some sentences and count how many different words are in those sentences.

66

1.) _____

 _____

2.) _____

 _____

3.) _____

 _____

4.) _____

 _____

5.) _____

 _____

6.) _____

 _____

7.) _____

 _____

Mentally Count the Words

67

Count and write how many different words there are in the given sentences.

1.) Animals need food for their growth and energy. _____

2.) Little Kelly came home from school. _____

3.) I have a horn on my head. _____

4.) How do plants act as air purifiers? _____

5.) The leaf is an essential part of a plant. _____

6.) Snakes swallow their prey. _____

7.) Dogs can tear flesh with their pointy teeth. _____

Mentally Count the Words

Count and write how many different words there are in the given sentences.

68

1.) She decided to tell her friends. _____

2.) Some birds live in very cold regions. _____

3.) Beaks and claws help birds to catch their food. _____

4.) Food can be cooked by boiling in water. _____

5.) Polly was invited to Jack's birthday party. _____

6.) Miles is a kind and courageous boy. _____

7.) Land animals generally walk on four legs. _____

Omit a word in a Sentence

What would remain if we removed the 3rd word from the sentence?

1. What hapened to Herry during the race?

   What hapened Herry during the race?

2. I won a prize in dance competition.

   _____

3. Everyone in the school seemed very excited.

   _____

4. The guest had already arrived.

   _____

5. The incident showed a new way to save the trees.

   _____

6. The princess is very beautiful.

   _____

7. To be ready to do something.

   _____

Omit a word in a Sentence

What would remain if we removed the 3rd word from the sentence?

1. She is waiting for the train.
   _____

2. Kelly is sitting with her mother.
   _____

3. Herry stood under the roof.
   _____

4. He was looking for his glasses.
   _____

5. He is talking to his friend.
   _____

6. The police came after the accident.
   _____

7. Is there anyone in the room?
   _____

Omit a word in a Sentence

What would remain if we removed the 3rd word from the sentence?

1. The cat ran after the rat.
   _____

2. She fell to the ground.
   _____

3. My mother prays to God everyday.
   _____

4. She was rewarded with a gold medal.
   _____

5. He sat besides me.
   _____

6. Is there anyone in the hotel?
   _____

7. I am waiting for the train.
   _____

Omit a word in a Sentence

What would remain if we removed the 3rd word from the sentence?

1. The sun was shining brightly.
   _____

2. My brother serves in the army.
   _____

3. Kelly eats ice-cream.
   _____

4. The man and his wife were working in their kitchen.
   _____

5. He made fun of his younger sister.
   _____

6. Do not go near the fire.
   _____

7. I went with my friends to the movies.
   _____

Substitute a word in a Sentence

73

What would remain if we substituted the 3rd word of the sentence with the word "cot".

1. Dolphin is not a fish.

   Dolphin is cot a fish.

2. I am a good dancer.

3. This is my favourite place.

4. She is a very good girl.

5. What did the young man become?

6. The teacher reads a magazine.

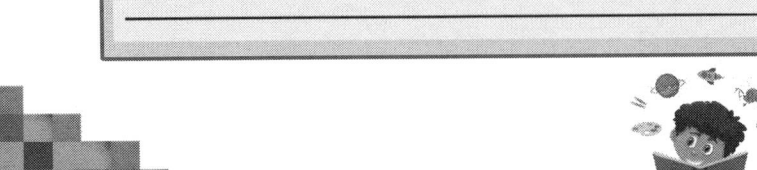

Substitute a word in a Sentence

What would remain if we substituted the 3rd word of the sentence with the word "blue".

1. The bicycle needs new lines.
   _____

2. We had a picnic in the garden.
   _____

3. She was going to the party.
   _____

4. He is present in the class.
   _____

5. I am very talkative.
   _____

6. This game is very expensive.
   _____

Substitute a word in a Sentence

75

What would remain if we substituted the 3rd word of the sentence with the word "pair".

1. You can play basketball.
   _____

2. I am late today.
   _____

3. Polly is a pretty girl.
   _____

4. I like fairy tales.
   _____

5. My favourite color is blue.
   _____

6. Two cats chased each other across the garden.
   _____

Substitute a word in a Sentence

What would remain if we substituted the 3rd word of the sentence with the word "stop".

1. The new satellite launched successfully.
   _____

2. It is a holiday tomorrow.
   _____

3. We will go on a picnic next month.
   _____

4. She is a beautiful princess.
   _____

5. I have a big soft toy.
   _____

6. My brother loves me very much.
   _____

Separate phrases into Words

Separate the words in the sentences with lines.

Idrinkmilkeveryday.

I / drink / milk / everyday.

Thecowgivesusmilk.

Mymotherbakescupcakesforme.

Myolderbrotherplaysfootballatthepark.

Theteacherteachesintheclass.

Ireadthenewspaperdaily.

Separate phrases into Words

Separate the words in the sentences with lines.

Mygrandfathertookmetotheparty.

_____

Icutmy15thbirthdaycake.

_____

Ibrushmyteethtwiceaday.

_____

Thegardenerwaterstheflowers.

_____

Kidsareplayingintheswimmingpool.

_____

Ilovetoplaywithmyyoungersister.

_____

Separate phrases into Words

Separate the words in the sentences with lines.

Jackisourclassmonitor.

_____

Shewasherelastmonth.

_____

Ihaveabeautifuldoll.

_____

Theyareallfootballplayers.

_____

Mileswashelpfultohisfriends.

_____

Mybrotherhastwocars.

_____

Separate phrases into Words

Separate the words in the sentences with lines.

Theteacherhasanewwoodentable.

Whathaveyoudonetoday?

Iblameherforit.

KellyandMarkarestudying.

Theyarethebeststudentsintheirschool.

Areyoucomingwithme?

Binomial sentences

Write sentences with the binomial " sick and tired ".

I am sick and tired of working long hours for little pay.

Binomial sentences

Write sentences with the binomial " short and sweet ".

Binomial sentences

Write sentences with the binomial " odds and ends ".

Binomial sentences

Write sentences with the binomial "back and forth".

Spelling exercises for Words

Read, spell and write the words.

- Read it
- Spell it aloud
- Write it twice

Word		Write it twice
become	✓	become become
agree	☐	_____ _____
bring	☐	_____ _____
cooked	☐	_____ _____
winter	☐	_____ _____
final	☐	_____ _____
choose	☐	_____ _____
greater	☐	_____ _____

Spelling exercises for Words

Read, spell and write the words.

86

- Read it
- Spell it aloud
- Write it two times

Read it	Spell it aloud	Write it two times
forget	☐	_____ _____
jumping	☐	_____ _____
reach	☐	_____ _____
swim	☐	_____ _____
forgotten	☐	_____ _____
shaken	☐	_____ _____
grown	☐	_____ _____
hurting	☐	_____ _____

Spelling exercises for Words

Make and write compound words.

foot	+	print	= footprint
high	+	way	=
post	+	man	=
loud	+	speaker	=
rain	+	drop	=
out	+	door	=
neck	+	tie	=
moon	+	light	=
your	+	self	=
grass	+	hopper	=

Spelling exercises for Words

Make and write compound words.

88

head	+	light	=	
car	+	go	=	
dish	+	cloth	=	
corn	+	ball	=	
can	+	did	=	
egg	+	shell	=	
earth	+	worm	=	
tool	+	box	=	
space	+	ship	=	
play	+	room	=	

Activity with Rhymes

Read the word and write the word that rhymes with it.

bake	take
freeze	
fly	
lose	
sing	
shake	
drink	
feel	
jump	
meet	
hot	

Activity with Rhymes

Read word and write the word that rhymes with it.

throw	
sleep	
wet	
wise	
hope	
germ	
write	
think	
wake	
flow	
cries	

Activity with Rhymes

Find and mark rhyming words.

rang	race	(hang)	steal	call
find	wet	quail	kind	walk
but	cut	frog	gone	pick
fall	tall	shell	book	class
kill	save	done	hope	till
swim	trim	duck	fish	cow
catch	stop	bake	there	match
do	well	yes	no	where
cap	man	map	vase	kite
blow	flow	egg	bite	fight

Activity with Rhymes

Find and mark rhyming words.

get	yes	wet	wise

hear	near	back	far

sell	lamp	cheap	bell

gate	mate	fast	gone

food	close	have	mood

right	fight	class	must

win	fan	bin	dark

teach	here	reach	close

phone	tone	fell	mice

throw	fair	rice	crow

92

Scrabble type Letters

Solve the color Word Search.

RED	GREEN	YELLOW
BLUE	ORANGE	PURPLE

R	E	D	N	H	Y	U	I	O	P
Q	A	S	D	F	G	J	I	B	B
X	Z	R	T	P	U	R	P	L	E
H	Y	J	K	L	B	F	R	U	M
D	C	V	B	T	U	S	W	E	A
Y	I	Y	E	L	L	O	W	F	N
S	D	F	T	U	I	N	M	J	C
X	Q	A	U	I	O	P	M	F	R
D	X	O	R	A	N	G	E	C	N
S	B	I	O	D	E	R	A	X	M
V	G	T	I	D	K	E	A	J	K
Z	D	C	Y	I	S	E	E	R	D
V	B	U	I	Q	A	N	C	F	T

Scrabble type Letters

Solve the shape Word Search.

| CIRCLE | SQUARE | OVAL |
| TRIANGLE | STAR | HEART |

T	R	I	A	N	G	L	E	Q	I
G	R	F	B	N	K	I	S	W	C
A	X	J	L	V	F	R	Y	U	I
F	K	L	R	D	M	Z	A	Q	R
T	G	B	K	I	C	D	F	G	C
E	X	J	K	O	P	S	A	W	L
V	M	K	N	S	Q	U	A	R	E
O	F	A	Y	T	W	Q	A	K	V
V	R	Z	V	A	D	B	U	I	Z
A	H	E	A	R	T	Q	W	Y	U
L	O	P	Z	X	V	B	M	E	W
D	E	R	U	I	O	Q	A	V	G
N	J	K	L	R	F	G	T	S	Z

Scrabble type Letters

Solve the Crossword puzzle.

| NICE | PLAY | BATH |
| OPEN | HAPPY | LIGHT |

Scrabble type Letters

Solve the Crossword puzzle.

| PEOPLE | FUNNY | HOUSE |
| WORK | FLOW | OTHER |

F _ _ _ _

W O _ _

H

P _ _ _ _

Visual discrimination of Syllables

Look at the pictures and match with the correct beginning sound.

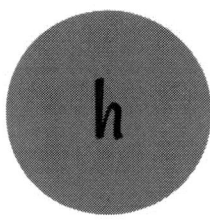 h 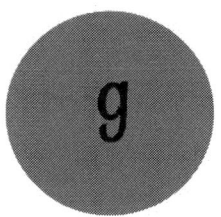 g
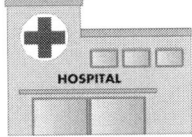

Visual discrimination of Syllables

Look at the pictures and match with the correct beginning sound.

98

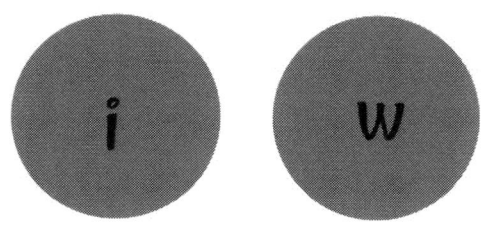

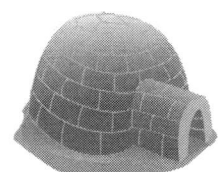

Visual discrimination of Syllables

Find and color the circles with the words that have a "ch" sound.

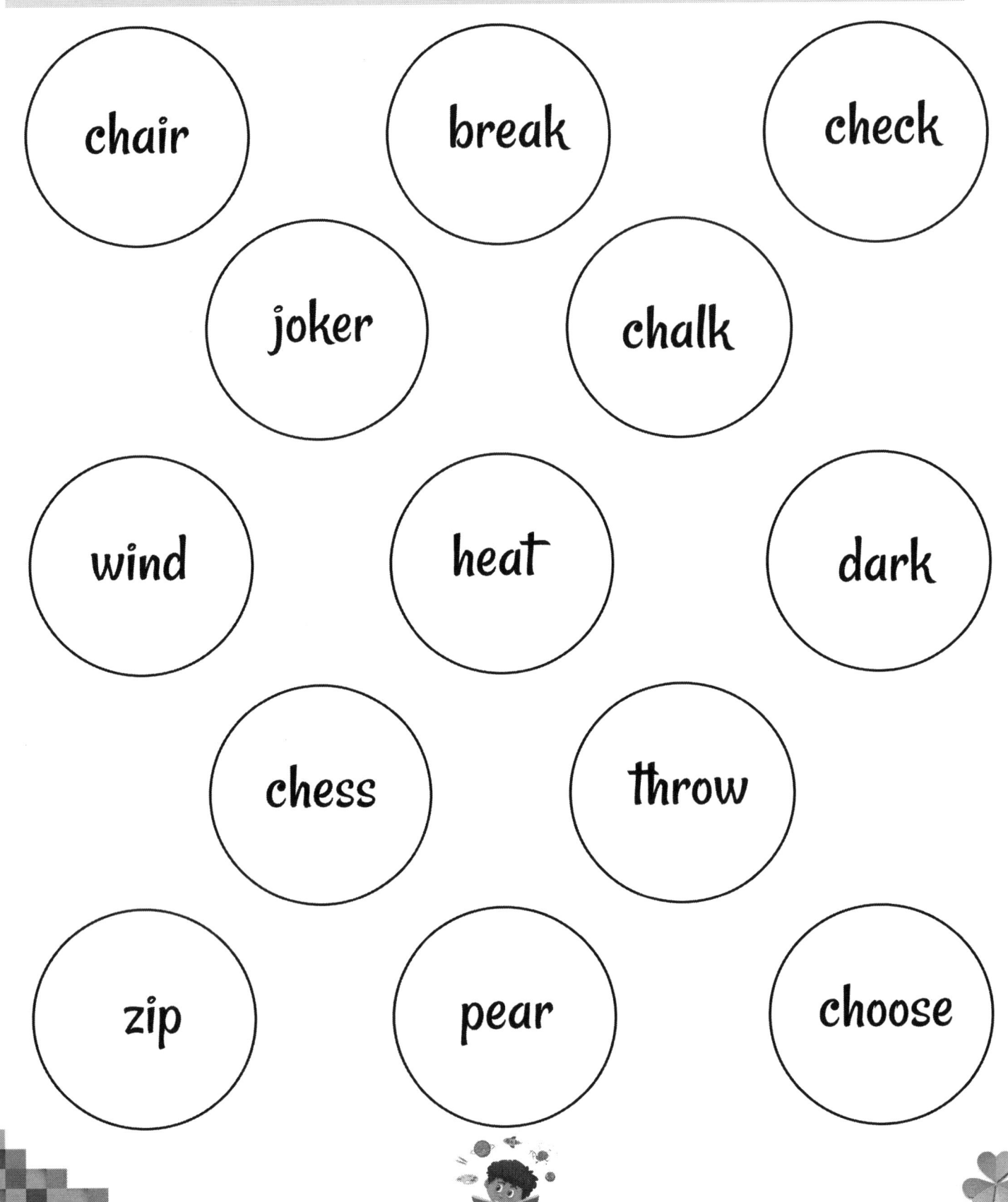

Visual discrimination of Syllables

Find and color the circles with the words that have a " wh " sound.

100

- whale
- shirt
- third
- white
- rice
- wind
- what
- whistle
- when
- shark
- while
- close
- wheat

Find the hidden sounds

Solution page 46: Write the hidden phoneme or letter that is missing in the word.

- is_o_metrics
- goosa_n_der
- deu_u_terium
- kidne_y_
- insta_n_ce
- deter_m_inable
- mati_o_ned
- p_u_rification

Find the hidden sounds

Solution page 47: Write the hidden phoneme or letter that is missing in the word.

102

bri_g_adier

st_r_eam

comma_n_ding

pect_o_ralis

additiona_l_

hormon_a_l

mo_i_sture

e_x_pelled

Ordering of Graphemes

Solution page 53: Order the letters to form a word.

taolt → total	dnxei → index
stra → star	ecipe → piece
rmka → mark	vserei → service
abcled → cabled	ulipbc → public

Ordering of Graphemes

Solution page 54: Order the letters to form a word.

pcabela → capable	rmof → form
vediesc → devices	mvoree → remove
tsnoe → stone	ergat → great
lpnat → plant	cxudlee → exclude

Ordering of Graphemes

Solution page 55: Order the letters to form a word.

ounsd → sound	hrbus → shrub
inev → vein	emnelte → element
srgap → grasp	vaido → avoid
csepea → escape	knsi → skin

Ordering of Graphemes

Solution page 56: Order the letters to form a word.

oels → sole	iulbd → build
ortnf → front	afel → leaf
esvarle → several	aseir → raise
ffero → offer	enalmt → mental

Printed in Great Britain
by Amazon